Crane
ABU-SUFYAN

LONDON
HERTFORDSHIRE PRESS
2016

Published in United Kingdom
Hertfordshire Press Ltd © 2016

9 Cherry Bank, Chapel Street
Hemel Hempstead, Herts.
HP2 5DE, United Kingdom

e-mail: publisher@hertfordshirepress.com
www.hertfordshirepress.com

CRANE
by ABU-SUFYAN ©
English

Edited by David Parry
Translated from Russian by Vasily Lakhonin
Design by Aleksandra Vlasova
Project manager Anna Lari

All rights reserved. No part of this book may be reprinted or reproduced or utilised in any form or by any electronic, mechanical, or other means, now known or hereafter invented, including photocopying and recording, or in any information storage or retrieval system, without permission in writing from the publishers.

British Library Catalogue in Publication Data
A catalogue record for this book is available from the British Library
Library of Congress in Publication Data
A catalogue record for this book has been requested

ISBN 978-1-910886-23-6
RRP: £ 12.50

Crane

We are responsible for animals before God!
It is written in the heavens.

Part 1

The golden sun smiled.
Leaves started shining on a pine tree,
A flock of cranes flew
To a native lake in spring.

It is a joyous time,
It is time for the cranes mating display.
Divine birds' of a large tribe
This catches every moment of spring days.

In the middle of a lake - wildlife sanctuary,
Is an island of swampland.
It is noisy there today, as at a feast.
The cranes are currently building nests.

Female cranes are pleased with themselves,
Having already loved their chicks.
They are hatching eggs silently,
While patiently rushing time.

Everyone is willingly doing their job,
Despite the coldest winds whistling.
Warming these eggs with their warm bodies…
All of them having about five or six eggs.

Yet, the crane nicknamed "Roza"
Has only one. Although, a very big egg.
So, Roza sheds tears from misery.
Wrinkling her little crane's face.

Endless sluggish days pass.
There is no time for rest here
And chicks are hatching,
Gifting these birds for their considerable pains.

Sadly, ill-fated Roza has no chick.
So, she does not know what to do.
Her thick-shelled egg is so firm,
The chick cannot break the egg.

Nestling wrecks the eggshell, wearily.
The mother hears a long: "Knock-Knock-Knock".
The crane stands over her egg,
While beating ancient sounds with her beak:

"I ask you, my baby, break through.
Strengthen yourself, as it is your time.
I would break it, but I'll crack the shell.
Hurry, you will hatch soon".

But, it is all for nothing.
Her chick cannot crack the shell!
Frankly, it feels sorry for that crane,
Because, he doesn't know what else can be done.

Roza cannot hear her baby anymore.
Her nestling has stopped knocking.
So she cries, streaming a tear;
Saying: "Do you hear me, my tomboy?

Oh, I'll find another lake,
So you can thence breathe better.
I just beg you - hatch, please!
Knock if you are still alive".

But sadly, there is no knocking,
Baby crane has fallen silent.
Sadness and sorrow gnaws at mother.
Even God will not help her.

She still lives as a captive of hope,
Since she cannot stop warming her burden.
She sits on her nest as before,
Willing life in her egg to endure.

She sat all that summer.
Bathed in the tears of an unfulfilled hope.
She lowered her head to somewhere
Wherein abounded rumours and ignorance.

Watching, Roza sees baby cranes everywhere.
Other mothers have thriving chicks.
All small feathered "guys"
Trying to fly to every corner.

Eventually, the crane clearly understood.
No one was alive in her egg.
It became offensive to her.
It became a source of sorrow.

Saddened, she stood up in her nest
Although dazed, as if from a dream:
And circling and stumbling:
Drank her bowl of grief to the dregs.

She saw the egg becoming black…
Emotions swirling in this bird's forehead!
But she braced up and bit the bullet, boldly.
Breaking through the shell with her beak.

At last, her egg broke up,
Having revealed the poor chick therein.
Then squeakily, her voice trailed off:
Observing the unborn chick's lifeless body.

"You're so big, so beautiful", said she,
"Each eye burning like an asterisk …
You will be handsome above all things",
The crane lamented, while crying.

Yet, sadly, life is cruel under the sky,
Sometimes hitting below the belt.
The sky quietly sobs, although from the East
A golden autumn is coming.

Preparing, therefore, for a long flight,
The cranes gathered to journey onwards -
Cranes with their kids breaking into formation
And leaving this island of earth.

Only Roza is unhurried in her departure
Standing beside her desolate nest.
She thought she heard orphans crying,
Beneath the weeping of tragic stars.

At last, the cranes ascended skyward.
Even though she spun over and over her nest-
Her wings flapping like black shrouds
Before the menacing long road ahead.

Part 2

White birches are in white boots.
My homeland is blasted by snow.
As cranes flee from the cold,
Flying far away to a distant land...

Spending their days there, under southern skies,
Where it is always warm, as in May.
While whistling blizzards are here on this island,
Having covered the lake with thick ice.

Imperceptibly, time passed.
Wild Nature departing as from a dream.
But, when winter blizzards have faded away,
Spring will have finally returned.

Having gathered in the sky, the tired flock
Glides - moving with manifold wings.
The cranes are speeding to the small island,
Where they'll find native land.

The inspired Roza is rushing:
Is flying ahead - breaking formation;
She lands on the island first,
Having found her little corner.

It is a joyous time!
It is time for the crane's mating display.
Divine birds' - large tribe,
Catching every moment in spring days.
The cranes are busy with their jobs.
All - as usual with these birds
Warm the eggs with their bodies.
Everyone has five or six eggs.

Only poor Roza is different:
She has one egg again!
This crane is crying in desperation:
She lost face once more.

"Is it possible", the poor thing thinks,
That my chick will die as before?"
It is difficult for her under these skies,
To imagine a weeping star shining for her.

Anyway, she hopes to get lucky!
She continues to heat her package,
Having calmed, she no longer cries,
Although, anxiety cools the gut.

Days are passing gloomily and sad.
Time crawls like a lame bug.
But, the Gods of our Universe have not slept.
Her chick is hitting its shell with his beak!

"There" - said Roza – finally,
My star begins to shine…"
Yet, flustered with happiness,
She struts importantly near her nest.

Meanwhile, breaking through the shell,
Her chick showed up.
So, covering him by herself,
Mother calmed down finally.

She forgot all her worries -
Life is happy…
And in heaven, where the Gods are feasting,
A chick's star has risen.

She worries over the chick, poor youngling:
She's got only the One!
Making it heavy to see the others…
Form a heavenly throng behind each mother.

Nevertheless, weeks were passing quickly.
And the chicks have rapidly fledged,
And having forgotten their beds,
Are trying to fly in every direction.

Each chick has grown up a miracle,
And Roza's chick has grown up too.
He has became fun and beautiful...
After his mother's character.

The crane is proud of her baby.
And lived only for this godling...
And tirelessly prayed to this divinity,
She looked after him as best she could.

But the chick was very curious.
He stuck his nose in everywhere.
He even broke his wing - little silly
Not being responsive to mother's tears.

Becoming depressed, or desperate,
Roza found no rest through him:
Nor permanent happiness under the sky.
Only a continual, yet distant, hope.

Seeing the other chicks
Starting to fly over lowlands,
Roza wept... arguing with heavy Fate,
While trying to raise her chick's wing.

But unfortunately, this idea proved useless.
His wings do not flap or flip.
So, Roza disengaged with her life –
Roza had no luck in life thereafter…

Part 3

The birches rustled in the wind.
Their sap stopped flowing under the crust.
The golden autumn came -
East breathed its cool upon the land.

Preparing for their long flight,
The cranes gathered for their journey.
The cranes with younglings flying in formation,
Leaving this island of earth.

Only our Roza with her baby crane
Remained to hibernate in isolation.
Staying with her child,
She whiled away her care-heavy days.

The severe frosts came,
Making everything sleep under crystalline ice.
Yet, Roza felt an undiminishing woe:
There was no food – all around was frozen.

The chick cried:
"Give me something to eat.
It is cold and dreary…
We will die staying here."

The chick's voice hurried mom.
Roza tried to get worms:
Poking at the ground obstinately
She broke the tips of her claws.

Her chick runs after its mother-
To eat something finally.
But there is no food, only suffering.
Her nestling cries quiet in the wind.

Yet, mother is walking and swinging…
Albeit truly exhausted.
Meandering and sad, Roza with baby,
Rove across frost without food or sleep.

It was a long way …
Suddenly in front of them - a hut is a few steps away!
And they, like dear friends,
Hurried, having overcome anxiety.

Roza paused at the gate
And entered after knocking.
Her tired chick trudging behind her,
Dragging his wings in the snow.

Instantly, a dog jumped out barking
And attacked the chick.
But mother protecting the baby,
By waving and beating her wings a hundred times.

Fortunately, out of the hut
Ran the host himself: an old fisherman.
He kenneled the dog
Enchaining it securely.

And coming to these strange aliens,
He took the chick in his arms.
And driven by half-drunk airs,
He quickly led his guests into the house.

He fed and watered them - becoming their ambulance.
Keeping them in a warm corner,
And attended a wound
On the chicks left wing, carefully.

And having corrected broken bones,
Imposed rigid bandages on every gash.
His guests spun around in gratitude,
Even though the chick's wing ached.

They comfortably lived with the man,
Not knowing of fears or woes.
Nor grudges, neither hidden, or explicit,
Their host pleased them as he could.

So, the days passed ... and time healed.
The chick started beating its wing.
And spring days were coming soon -
The sun started shining outside their window.

Imperceptibly, weeks passed by.
Nature awoke from her sleep,
And winter blizzards faded away,
The spring had come finally.
And long-awaited flock of cranes
Would appear in the blue haze soon.
And the fisherman set
His dear guests free.

Waving with wings,
Roza finally departed with the cranes…
May they not fail, oh God!

14.03.2012

Mother

A Modern ballad

We proposed a toast at weddings
And we glorified our mothers with words,
In the meantime, others living are forgotten by children.
My father used to say.

Having left a lonely mother,
Having easily left his native home,
Her son had gone way
Looking for happiness in a foreign land.

And he started a new life there
By projecting his hot-tempered eagerness,
And diving into its dashing depths,
Until he had forgotten about his mother.

And his old mother in her village
Was left alone without relatives.
Or welfare — Only a hut, trees,
And firewood. With the road as well as the moon.

The old woman worked as before.
She lived, offended by Fate.
Building sweet hopes,
But dripping tears in the night.

She cried speechless - asking God,
To keep her son from harm.
Often going along the road.
"Waiting for her son" - as The Poet wrote.
But her son was never there.

"Is it real, — this poor creature thought
That he has disappeared from our World?
Or, driven by heavy desires,
He doesn't want to see me anymore?

Is he walking hungry in the dark,
Alone, with sadness in his soul?
Nothing warms on a cold day
When there is nobody to see anything?

My son – my only joy!
Did he die in a foreign land?
If not, surely he would have come home,
To embrace his mother".

Yet, mother still lives with the hope
That her son will come back:
She tailors his clothes in the middle of the night.
Clothes he had never worn…

Year after year, she lived this way.
Time crept slowly.
And life flowed on in the usual way,
But the horizon was as empty as before.

Because of such grievances
Ailments stuck to her like misfortunes.
She went blind. Became demoralized:
She was so unlucky with her son!

But neighbors, thank goodness...
Are truly kind
Caring for her day by day,
Making the planet a kinder place.

So, she lives, not angry, nor repenting,
Eking a life out of Fates wheel.
Walking around the house, stumbling,
Feeling everything by touch.

Yet, sitting by her hearth for a long time,
Although she can't see anything
(And in old thin cape)
She waits for the wanderer.

She dreams that her son is over the hills.
But having lost his way on the road,
And will call for mother's help in the night:
Groaning in his chest.

Whiling away her days
Being a captive of dreams,
She sits alone, blind,
Having lost all connection to Earth.

Yet, her inner voice whispers,
"He will come back to his father's house,
And my life will be easier soon,
And light will begin to shine in blind eyes.

And spheres will revolve in the sky,
And life will wake up at home again.
And a string of happy days
Will help me to become healthy."

But life is violent with her.
She neither knows where her son is,
Nor why she sits alone
Under a high acacia tree.

Mother does not know what to do–
Her soul is exhausted!
The tragedy of her life lasts endlessly,
So, each day passes slowly.

Suddenly a miracle comes true.
On a wonderful warm day
There, as if from nowhere,
A car beeps to her.

And she hears her son's voice–
His words, his steps…
It is like the sky has split,
And a warm look enters her eyes.

She stands up stumbling
Goes to the voice... but on the way
No wanderer takes her in an embrace.
But a child - like an angel - in the flesh!

"Granny" says her granddaughter
"Fate has heeded your plea!
Please, scold Dad
For driving you to despair"

Then silence fell,
A hiatus pausing each moment;
Like sunlight from supreme will
A long desired peace came into the house.

She dissolved in the hands of her granddaughter -
This old woman in a headscarf.
And her granddaughter leaned down silently
Clung to her grandmother's hand.

Then grandmother (having calmed down),
Drooped her sad head
And bowed from the waist,
To her much-valued guest...

She touched her face gently.
Stroked her kindly.
Kissing the granddaughter ... inconsolably,
And got teary with happiness.

Kissing the granddaughter again:
"You look like me" she said.
A grandmother's gilded cloud
Appearing at the end of the day".

"Tell me, Mom, what is wrong with your eyes? –
The son asks being so sad. –
"I do not know. I don't like doctors.
The Lord alone knows it."

The entire world was enveloped by darkness
Like all of my nightly nights...
There was no escape for me anywhere:
There were no loved ones next to me,—

So, son said to his mother,
Concealing the pain in his feelings.
"I forgot my greatest debt" —
(Adopting a sheepish tone)
"I wandered through the world endlessly-
I'm guilty before you;
I wandered around like a bum,
I knocked at doors inopportunely.

I found a refuge in the world,
On the fifth floor.
Where we live in a two-room apartment;
With family – as you understood.

I have a wife and children ...
And a prized eldest daughter-
But among the stars atop our world,
You are the only one, Mom!

Having forgotten for a moment about my cares,
I came back, mother, for you.
I have accommodation; work...
And henceforth you will live with me." –

Mother replied, "I'll not go to a noisy city,
To live in a fifth floor flat.
I have been used to wide spaces since childhood,
They calm my very soul;

And fortunately, you have children...
So, don't feel sorry if I die.
Now, son, I know where you are -
I won't grieve anymore hereafter.

The neighbors are helping me here...
I can do housework by myself:
I know where everything is by heart-
I haven't taken leave of my senses."

So, mother answered son.
Without thinking twice. Then,
Concealing all of her sorrows,
She conducted her guests through the old house.

They were walking, eating, singing in chorus
The shadow of sadness disappeared.
Yet, two weeks passed by quickly,
And the day of departure came.

Dropping tears, mother said:
"I wish you a safe trip.
Upon your arrival send a telegram...
Go in peace. May the Lord bless and keep you!"

Then, the car started moving,
And son bent down to the wheel.
His girl cried behind a window:
"I love you grandmother!

I'm not giving up on you, grandmother!
I'll come again in the summer;
I will take dad with me too...
Do not cry, my grandmother!"

But the voice of her loved ones soon ceased,
Becoming weaker and weaker.
Until it seems this relationship
Between these three disappeared again.

Grandma cries at the gate –
She is upset again.
And in her old thin robe
She still sits alone.

Mare

The prolongation of one's kind is the meaning of life,
This is our natural immortality
The postulate of biology.

The long road collects dust:
A mare runs on a trail,
Her foal is running after her.
Their road is long under a hot sun.

Thirst drives them to a watering hole,
The earth itself groans from the heat,
The air in the sky burns as a flame,
This pathetic aridity is cruel.

Rivers and lakes have dried out
Around and under their gaze.
Where they will find water to drink,
The mare doesn't know.

Dust penetrates their eyes and ears.
But, the horse is supporting her foal.
With her tongue
As mother bears up her child:

A little longer… behind that prairie,
Where the heights stretch like a chain,
A creek flows under an oak.
There they can drink water.

These bleary horses -
Anticipating the taste of sweet moisture,
Run briskly, but tired
To the little oak.

Finally, there is the oak.
But where is the loquacious stream?
From the believed-in brook,
Only dry ground remains.

And the mare sheds tears
Asking her baby to drink:
"Taste my salty tears,
They are cooler then freezing cold waters"

The foal hurries to her mother,
Like a thirsty child in expectation.
And tenderly licks at her tears,
All transparent like dew in the morning.

The mare is desperate,
But she cannot accept her fate
Although, they are even more thirsty.
Yet, there are no clouds under these eternal skies.

Only dust penetrating their eyes and ears.
But, this horse supports her foal
With a tongue
As a mother bears up her own child.

"I know that behind those mountains
There is a spring under a rock.
Shall we run there until night?
That rock is not so far from here.

The narrow path is dusty:
And the mare is running and tired.
Her foal wobbles after her -
Their way is long under this hot sun.

The exhausted horses
Anticipating the sweet taste of moisture,
Are running, pacing, but tired.
It is a little too far to the spring.

Their path leads them along a slope.
And the foal who is distant from mom
Shouts, "It is hard for me to go quickly
On such a stony track"

"A little more - still a little more -
And you will get the hang of this road.
Faster, faster, my sheet lightning"-
So the mare answered.

Already in front of them, sideways lying,
Each rock gets dark with black moss.
But the promised cool spring
Had already been drunk by ruthless heat.

With no place for empty resentments.
The horse with her own hoof
Tried digging a deeper groove ...
But only silt was down below.

Having seen this slush, her foal
Hurried to drink like a child.
Yet, having drunk a sip of the damned sand,
Whinnied in a squeaky vexation.

The mare was so tired.
But didn't dare to expire,
Instead, she supported her foal,
As a mother bears up her child:

"Hold on, baby, don't despair.
To spite the Devil and scary spirits,
We will find the life-giving source of water.
It's out there - and I know where, exactly.

In a cave behind that mountain
(After an hour of walking, I have to say)
An underground river flows.
One there, we can enjoy water.

* * *

The dusty path:
A mare is running hard,
Her foal is running after her.
Their road seems longer under a hot sun.

Treeless territories abound -
Unusually beautiful, as in a fairy tale.
But burning hot nature
Has craved rain for six months.

These weary horses,
Anticipating the taste of sweet moisture,
Hurry up, running - then go slowly.
It is a little further to the cave.
Like the jaw of an unknown beast,

The hollow is already to be seen -
Nature's wonderful creation,
And breathing with a cool breath.
The mare came into a cave.

She runs inside about thirty meters,
Fearing as a mother for her child.
Then she calls her foal.
Into its fantastical vaults,

There are icicles, crystals, rocks.
There are underground networks of labyrinths,
Such as no one can find in the world.
But where is the desired water?

The mare has become weakened -
Stumbling more than once.
She swayed from thirst.
She stood and saw with a flaming gaze.

At the bottom of a large, dry, bowl,
She noticed a mirror of water,
And hurried down there to drink.

Yet, this water glistens like three eyes.
Not being enough for three sips.
The horse, having spread her hooves,
Suddenly breathed out deathlessly,

She wanted to drink water,
But then came round:
Since her foal was thirsty-
Her only child.

So, not wishing to be unkind,
The first and the last sip
She gifted her descendant
And started forgetting her thirst.

What about her kin? The foal,
The horse's skinny child,
Stood on legs like a heron,
Until he drank the last drop.

"Oh, mother", - the youngling said -
"I had only three sips,
But there is no more water,
And you didn't get even a drop."

In response, the mare hardly spoke:
"I didn't want a drink -
You quenched your thirst, thank God!
Now it's time to go"

Meanwhile, the mare's head
Was getting cloudy with thirst.
Trembling and shaking
Until she fell down on the hard ground beneath.

The foal neighed in a high-pitched manner
And cried pitifully, sadly:
"Oh mother, what is wrong with you?
What will happen to me without you?"

"My little one, my sheet lightning -
The mare cried out with love,-
You live under the shadow of the sky,
You are not without a tribe or clan.

Our herd is free and great,
Undomesticated and quite wild.
Your father, he is a frisky horse,
He is tall, white, gold-maned.

You were small and thin, and sick –
Our leader was displeased -
And I fell behind the herd,
Waiting until you became stronger.

Well, the rest you know.
Now, I hope you understand,
You're not just a foal,
You are descended from gold-mane!

That's why your mane is bright.
You are handsome, like your father.
But, I have no strength to go on.
Do not hurry - there is no night.

Do not be afraid. You're a grown-up.
You will go to the west across valleys.
There, our herd is waiting at the river,
Walking freely without a bridle."

Then, the mare became ill:
She stopped breathing.
The foal cried above her for a long time
He stood and cried like a child.

A long dusty road:
The mare no longer runs up the road-
Yet, the orphaned foal is running.
And his way will be long under the sun…
Very long.

07.10.1993

The Golden Shoes

The golden shoes

Masha went to the forest for mushrooms.
And gathering a basketful there,
She walked, rambling, along outlandish trails.
Losing her way in the dark forest.

She was straggling for a long time,
But, kept her anxiety in a young heart.
Unnoticed, suddenly, a big hut appeared:
Playing with wreaths of homespun fire.

Among dense age-old trees
A small glade was also seen!
But, without human inhabitants,
The hut merely took a nap.

Who lived or slept there?
Almost getting scared,
She quietly approached the hut,
And opened its big oak door.

Within its empty quietude,
No people could be found.
Only the stove burning famously,
And God keeping His silence.

But everything else was unkempt,
Everything here and there: everywhere dirty.
Yet, if there were no people dwelling therein,
How did it become dirty?

It's unclear who stoked the fire?
Who was lying on the large coach?
Why was this hut so dirty,
Why doesn't it shine with purity?

Our Masha started singing quietly:
"My hosts will come back soon…
So, I will hit the ground running,
Scrubbing and scouring everything".

She then cleared things from the table,
Swept and moped the floors,
Tidied up blankets on the ottoman
And quickly cleaned the shelves.

She saw that the stove had less fire,
And there is no food in the pantry…
But, she prepared a marvelous dinner,
From the mushroom's she had collected.

Baking bread from flour,
Squeezing juice from berries …
She set the table without any problem,
So that everyone could taste this feast.

Yet, time persisted and passed.
And the sun set over the hill.
Before somebody`s shadow finally darkened,
The round window like a stormy cloud.

Masha quickly hid behind the stove,
She felt a little scared.
She fell silent like a lamb.
Although, courageous from her birth

She looked furtively from behind the stove,
Looking at the door as it opened,
While a blustering beast unexpectedly entered
And came instantly into the hut.

Clumsily, a shaggy bear observed the girl
And started screaming.
As the two bears following him
Also screamed in choral anger.

But, they soon calmed down,
Once their attention was drawn
To the sparkling spaces within the hut
And the festive table before them.

Indeed, all three of them fell silent.
The elder rising on his hind legs
Saying, "Do not be afraid… from now
We are all the friends of destiny.

I assure you we won't touch you
We will let your life last for years!
To get started, show yourself at least…
And let's see each other in full view.

So, she is came out from her hiding place.
From behind the stove into sight.
And speaking with a thin voice began saying,
"I am so sorry bears for my impertinence.

I was lost in the woods…
And I entered your hut without asking.
But, I want to get home,
Even though the forest has darkened".

The eldest bear
"What is your name, young Lady?
And where do you come from?
Until now no human-people
Have ever been in a bear`s shelter".

Masha
"My name is Masha.
I am from the neighboring village…
I picked mushrooms in the midwood,
I accidentally found this hut".

The eldest bear
"I am a bear. I am Michael Topygin…
And with me is my wife.
This is our crying son,
He is the spitting image of me.

Our hut is clean and shining.
Thank you for tidying things.
But, tell me my darling one,
What do you want for this work"?

Masha
"I want nothing, uncle-Michael,
I just want to help you…
I am glad to be useful in life
And help everyone overcome their troubles.

Why is the little bear crying?
What happened to his pad?
It isn't for nothing this child is suffering"
Although, she saw nothing around him.

Topygin
"A barb penetrated deep under his nail,
We are unable to remove this splinter.
In order to not to whine with suffering,
He is ready to cut off his paw".

Masha
"Can I see the little bear?"
She spoke her words on the go,
As the girl inclined to the baby,
To obviate misfortune immediately.

She looked under its claw,
And saw a nail deep within.
An abscess covered the paw,
Making it difficult to remove the splinter.

So, she took a knife: heated it up,
Then dissected the abscess with skill.
She hooked-out the splinter with deft hands,
And striped it away with one sweep.

She put a bandage on the wound,
Finally calming down the pain,
And she said: "I will not preach …
But this is good for you young baby!"

Then the bears, delighted by Masha,
Started dancing and singing aloud:
"Since you have become a friend of ours
You will give you the title of hero".

Masha
"And now, I ask you, bears!
To sit down at this big table quickly,
And taste my meal all together.
You probably need to eat".

The procedures had all been followed
While their food she started to serve …
They praised her for her supper,
All of them bowing in turn.

Topygin
"Observing your old clothes,
We can see you are not rich,
Your sandals are broken…
You don't take care of your shapely legs.

But we appreciate your friendship and trust.
You wouldn`t leave your friends in trouble...
And the treasure of your soul - its riches-
Are found in your simple kindness".

Masha
"Probably, everybody is looking for me-
I have to go back home.
But in the forest devils are hissing,
And my path is hidden by darkness".

Topygin
"Do not be afraid of devils in the shadows.
If necessary, I will teach them a lesson.
Do not worry about your path:
I will give you a ride by myself".

Masha now rode on a bear,
Through the forest, in the night.
A young Lady rules cheerfully,
Those terrible beasts in the woods.

So, wandering under the starry dome,
Beneath a sad moon, while riding,
On a shaggy and terrible bear
She managed to got home.

Masha said, parting with her friend:
"I will continue to come to you"
And plucking a tear from her eyelashes,
She didn't know what to do.

Topygin
"Don`t worry, beautiful Lady!
I memorized the village and your house.
Now you have us bears…
And we will always be at your service".

Then the bear left with a jig,
And rearing onto his hind legs,
He walked through the forest (a little saddened),
But, overall happy about his luck.

Meeting her daughter,
Mother came out to the sill (shedding a tear).
Masha then started talking
About her adventure in the forest that night.

Her family were mad-keen on Masha,
Of her goodness of heart, they all spoke.
Even a moth flying in the sky,
Smiled from a great height above.

Yet, the young Lady got upset,
As from sin in sinless paradise.
She had forgotten her basket
Beneath the bear`s ottoman…

And she said, "I will go to them tomorrow,
And will tidy their room once again.
And I will certainly find my basket,
If I have good luck.

Meanwhile, it's far too late.
The horizon itself has dozed off.
Every midnight star is still whispering,
And Mary has visited each dream".

So, she fell asleep without waking,
After that long and stormy day.
Although, difficult to forget her adventures:
Her memories kept repeating their raptures.

And a clumsy bear - in her dreams -
Came knocking at her window that night;
He was waving to Masha with his huge paw,
Although, not roaring, rustling, or saying anything.

Masha was scared a little.
But, recognized Topygin soon.
So, she quietly opened the window,
To show her continuing friendship.

The bear approached very carefully.
And handing over her basket,
Bowed slightly, then departed.
He reared up keeping silent,

Even though waving back to his friend,
He went slowly into the woods.
Walking along an imaginary circle,
He was out of sight very soon.

Masha opened the basket -
And contrary to every night tale -
She was surprised (with mouth agape),
To see a new pair of shoes.

These shoes – they were not ordinary,
They shone like the sun - even in darkness.
Gold shoes, they were for her feet,
Like keys to a young girl's happiness.

Their separation was no more.
Her friend showed his unending thanks.
Masha was spinning with happiness,
Among the stars in her golden shoes.

But, even sweet dreams are not forever.
And like a crimson chime too quick,
This evening passed into history
As a fairy-dream that had gone-by.

Mary saw the morning hour was struck.
And the lightning sparkled on fire;
And the basket stood strange
On an open window ledge.

Blue flowers lay therein,
And under them, at the bottom,
There were the golden shoes,
She had worn in her sleep.

Their separation was overcome.
And because of these surprises.
Masha spun from happiness,
Among her friends in golden shoes.

30.12.2014.

Expectation

Cruelest Storms
Are raging above us.
We often create them
By negligent arms.
The tragedies of life
Sometimes, like a tsunami,
Destroy vital moments
In our home and our rest.

Part 1

In a distant village,
Where birches whisper,
She is living carefree.
The one girl.
She is blooming like
A rose under the sun.
She is shining with beauty,
As at midnight – like the moon.

She is just five years old.
And even though young,
People are already naming her
Sophia.

She lives with her mother
Under a squalid roof,
Unaware, fortunately,
How the years are running.

She is singing with her mother
Every child's song.
She is roaming with her friends,
In harmony with everything.

She is funny ... just
Like a heavenly angel.
And she pervades
Their lowly house.

Time is passing
Without sadness or thirst.
Until a Cherub,
Whispers to her in the night.
Yet, our Sofia
Got sad one day.
So, she stuck like glue to her mother
With a question:

"I won't be offended,
Tell me to my face.
Otherwise, how can I claim
Deafening fame?
All of my friends,
Have mothers and fathers...
But I have just one
Living without a daddy?"

Mother got upset,
Sorrowing seriously.
Although, she answered this fated insult:
"Do not cry, my sunshine!
Sooner or later,
I knew - you would ask me
Of this and that.

Your father has gone,
He is living abroad.
I do not know when he will be back.
But sooner or later
He will return
And will live with us
Under one roof."

Sofia
"I have never seen him, Mom
Please, show me his photo".

And mother showed her
That photo fine,
Which was taken
When he was living there.

Although they had to wend their way through life
cutting the storm
Sofia kissed the priceless picture.
Poor girl.
Yet, she shed tears from happiness

Sofia
"Can I, Mom,
Pray to you like to God,
While also loving daddy from now?
Oh, if he knew,
How I love him,
Probably he wouldn`t live there."

Mother
"Love your Dad,
Love until you drop.
Love him boundlessly,
I love him, too.
I have been waiting for him
Over these six years…
I`m patient,
But, I hurry up each day."

Sofia
"I advise you Mom,
To put away your tears.
Don`t worry.
Don`t be sad.
He will come soon.
The birches are whispering.
That he will come.
And I will await him too… "

Since then, everyday
Alone on the sill,
Sofia stood quite still,
Concealing her grief.
Even when climbing
The flat hill,
She looked up from there,
Into the long distances.

But, father wasn't there.
Not even a shadow.
Each road passing
Into empty horizons.
So, she waited,
Without crying or laziness,
On the hill day by day
Until she had sat a whole year.

So, time went by
Without great events.
The days passed by,
Like limping rabbits.
Until mother
Said to Sofia:
"Your dad has come…
Along with his wife!"

From such a shock
Sofia sat down.
Into her poor young head
A hazel got mixed.
So, not knowing what to do,
She turned pale
And suddenly started crying,
Hitting herself in the bosom.

Then mother hurried
To calm down her daughter.
And taking her in kindly arms
Kissed her,
Stroked her curls,
And said in gentle
Breaths of love:

"Under the everlasting sky
Nothing is haphazard.
But, your father knows nothing
About a child
Who was born in deepest secret.
Nothing about a child who came into this world
As his daughter.

You my daughter.
We aren`t married…
I wanted to make
A surprise for daddy.
Of course, it is my fault
That my whim turned in such a way".

Sofia
"When I meet father
Let me speak…
I will tell him every detail.
Letting my father know
I am existent.
And this will be revenge
On his unwelcome wife."

Mother
"Your father will hear
About his sweet daughter.
Rumours are loud
Among spinning gossips.
Let's not hurry
And force such talk.
And soon, finding everything out,
He will return by himself."

So, time went by,
One week after another…
And life under the moon
Pressurized each offence.
Until daughter Sofia,
And her lovely mother
Grew wild with desperation
Not knowing what to do.

Daddy didn't come.
Beloved didn't remember…
Because of this
Sofia`s mother fell ill.
And her life of crying
Under their dark cupola.
Wrapped them in a palace,
Of sadness and haze.

She got sick
From bitter resentment.
And lived in vain
In the hope of a meeting.
And her daughter grew up
Hating herself,
Although keeping her love
All through the years.

Sofia looked after mother
As best she could,
Yet, she was sad and cried often.
"My poor one.
God, please, take pity,
Be kind!
Omnipotent, God."

Part 2

Sofia decided
(Seeing her daddy)
To run after him
Behind mother's back.
She just wanted a fatherly hug,
Not thinking
About anybody.

So, she entered quietly
An unknown courtyard
As a door opened and creaked before her -
As a man in uniform walked out from there -
Having fun
With his wife.

She was confused,
Having seen these spouses.
Words stuck in her throat like a lump. .
The man bent over her
And said quietly:
"Are you looking for your home?"

Sofia
"I am not looking for my home…
Nor a high palace…
All these years and days
I have been looking for daddy."

The man
"I can strangely see
Your answer severe.
Please, tell me,
Who is your father?"

Sofia
"I recognized you at once
We have your photo.
My lovely father,
You are the one!"

The man
"Why was there silence about this
All these years?
What is your name young beauty?"

Sofia
"I am Sofia.
My mother's name is Catherine.
We have been waiting for you for five years daddy."

Then spouse Marina
Started speaking:
"It turns out that you, my darling,
Were married long ago."

Husband
"I met with Kate
Only twice.
And we weren`t married back then.
About this girl I neither knew nor heard
Can you be more understanding?"

Sofia
"My mother is ill
Staying in bed,
I look after her…
But it is hard to me!"
She cried in a state of delirium
For three weeks without end.
Unhappiness has fallen on her
Like fog."

Marina
"It happened just so,
There is nothing to do.
It is useless
To talk of the past.
It is better, darling,
To take up this matter,
And offer immediate help
To mother and daughter.

And then all three of them
Ran to the ill woman.
Poor Sofia
She led them by herself.
They come home.
They sympathized with Kate,
Yet, in her delirium, Kate didn't recognize them.

So, immediately to the hospital,
(That is in the district center),
They took her.
Hurrying time all the way.
Afterwards, hours passed by slowly
In a wakeful nightmare.
And Sofia cried still,
Kicking herself:

"I am not pleased by this worrisome life
My mother would be happy without a daughter.
Of course, it is my fault…
Yet, why was I born,
And why do I draw breath!"

She left with daddy
And Marina,
Covering anxieties about her mother.
She was leaving and suffering,
With a guilty soul,
As if she was walking

In a darkened forest.
Since then, everyday,
Sofia stood alone by the sill.
Dressed in sadness.
Even when going up the flat hill.
Looking from there
Into alarming distances.
But, mother isn`t there.
Not even a shadow
Passes on the roads.
So, hiding in the darkness.
She waits.
Crying without laziness
Sitting on the hill
Each day…

Times went by,
Without great events.
The days passed,
Like limping rabbits.
Every soul-error
Depressing her -
And the fact that her mother
Was driven by fate.

But, one usual day,
As Sofia went up the hill
With her pale expression
She saw the path to the road
Collecting new dust.
The Heavenly power
Wasn't taking a nap.

She could see from the hill
A familiar shadow
Within these unusual dusts.
She found her mother
Was hurrying along the way,
Having left her lazy illness in hospital.

Her head had already began to spin.
She couldn't wait any longer
For her mother over there.
So, Sofia stood up,
Lifted in spirits
And started running
Toward her mother.

These two native souls
Ran towards each other
Hurrying up hours -
While angels in the sky
Were spinning
And leading them
To a precious moment.

They were running, chipper,
Although running and feeling tired.
And, as if eternity,
In a moment lasts therein
(Even though but a little time
Remained before their meeting)
Sofia's mother
Was heard to scream:

"I am running my darling,
I am running, stumblingly…"
Sofia responded:
"Don't rush,
Since this is a moment
Wherein even awkwardly,
One soul is allowed to embrace another."

The Universe urgently
Became numb in two ticks -
Only their hearts,
Were knocking, whispering.
Mother and daughter
In the wide, wide, world
Were the only ones celebrating:
Almost too scared to shout.

Sofia
"Thoughts and thinking,
Now purposeful, no longer asleep.
I am thinking of my mother.
I am waiting for you, mother dear.
Day and night,
I sat on that hill
All the livelong day
On that lonely hill."

Mother
"We will live together from now onwards
But, we will also persuade daddy
To visit three times a day."

Sofia
"In order that we, at last,
Can live all three together,
I will marry them off by myself."

Marina heard similar words as rumours.
Yet, she took pity on
Mother and daughter.
Suddenly, therefore, she left.
Maria was sad, but without fault.
No one could condemn Marina.

Sofia twirled "all crazy" as a daughter.
Now, a matchmaker,
Not hiding her tears.
She married mother and father together,
Thereby bathing her family in happiness.

So, Sofia loved mother and father,
Calming down every heartache.
And in their two hearts
(Tied stubbornly with love —)
She was permitted her to play
A Heavenly role.

13.10.2015.

REVIEWS

Extrapolating larger themes from the people and creatures of which he writes, Abu-Sufyan's Crane speaks of the yearning, hope and finally acceptance inherent in life. Grounded in the earth, these eloquent poems tell of the changing of the seasons and ultimately the generations with the dreamlike, heart-wrenching quality of a fairy-tale.

— *Stephen M. Bland, writer*
United Kingdom

After reading this book, I felt that I became mentally clearer and wiser. Indeed, Abu –Sufyan is a poet whose poetry is vital reading for people at this difficult time!

— *Maksim Korsakov, writer*
Canada

Three poetic works ... Three stories told by the author in simple, clear language: "Crane", "Mare" and "Mother". Each of them telling its own story ... A story, which tells a mystery without mentoring, or giving directions, to the reader. Three stories about a mother's love: a mother's fate. Allowing one to feel the story line, but without a disclosed final concept. Indeed, the author makes the reader feel and think simultaneously.

— *Lenifer Mambetov, writer*
Prize-winner in the category of best female author in OEBF - 2014
Republic of Crimea

ABU – SUFYAN, a poet of great talent. His poems suit both children and adults.

— *Gulsifat Shahidi, journalist, PhD Philology, writer.*
Tajikistan

REVIEWS

The book of poems "Crane" – written in simple words and simple syllables. It is easy to read and pleasant to grasp. Certainly, Abu - Sufyan can hide in common words a strong sense of humanity in each of his poems.

— Uzakbaeva Cholpon
Kyrgyz-Russian Slavic University
Kyrgyzstan

The wisdom of Abu Sufyan is within his observations: within his ability to (skilfully) present a theme to his reader. Undoubtedly, he is able to see that not everyone will notice, or understand, his work.

— Bakhyt Rustemov,
Academician of International Eurasian Academy of TV, radio and media
Kazakhstan

CONTENTS

Crane	*4*
Mother	*18*
Mare	*28*
The Golden Shoes	*38*
Expectations	*51*